Marvel Studios'
Black Panther

Based on the Screenplay by
Ryan Coogler and Joe Robert Cole
Story by Stan Lee and Jack Kirby

Produced by Kevin Feige, p.g.a.
Directed by Ryan Coogler

Level 3

Retold by Lynda Edwards

Series Editors: Andy Hopkins and Jocelyn Potter

Pearson Education Limited

KAO Two

KAO Park, Harlow,

Essex, CM17 9NA, England

and Associated Companies throughout the world.

ISBN: 978-1-2923-4747-9

This edition first published by Pearson Education Ltd 2018

1 3 5 7 9 10 8 6 4 2

The authors have asserted their moral rights in accordance
with the Copyright Designs and Patents Act 1988

Set in 9pt/14pt Xenois Slab Pro

Printed by Neografia, Slovakia

Published by Pearson Education Limited

For a complete list of the titles available in the Pearson English Readers series, visit
www.pearsonenglishreaders.com.
Alternatively, write to your local Pearson Education office or
to Pearson English Readers Marketing Department,
Pearson Education, KAO Two, KAO Park, Harlow, Essex, CM17 9NA

MIX
Paper from
responsible sources
FSC™ C128612

Contents

Who's Who?

T'Challa

T'Challa is a prince of Wakanda with special powers. These make him strong. He can also jump and fight like a panther. He wants to stop his country's vibranium—a very strong metal—from falling into the wrong hands.

Nakia

Nakia was T'Challa's girlfriend, and is a Wakandan spy. She helps people who are suffering in other countries. She loves T'Challa. She also wants to be free to do her own work, though.

Okoye

Okoye is Wakanda's greatest warrior. She is a fierce fighter, and the head of the Wakandan guards. They look after the King and his family, and protect Wakanda from its enemies.

T'Chaka, Ramonda, and Shuri

T'Chaka (King of Wakanda) and Ramonda are T'Challa's parents. His sister, Shuri, is a very smart scientist. She has discovered many ways to use the country's vibranium in modern technology, weapons, and machines.

M'Baku

M'Baku is the leader of the mountain tribe, the Jabari. He and his people don't agree with the Wakandan way of life and never meet people from the other Wakandan tribes.

W'Kabi

W'Kabi is a friend of T'Challa's, and a Wakandan farmer. He and Okoye are in love, but have different opinions about uses of vibranium. In his opinion, Wakanda should use vibranium weapons to fight for poor African people around the world.

Everett K. Ross

Ross works for the CIA*. He has met T'Challa before, during an adventure with the Avengers. He knows about T'Challa's Black Panther powers, but not about the amount of vibranium in Wakanda. He is trying to find Ulysses Klaue.

Ulysses Klaue

Klaue is an international criminal, a thief, and a killer. He began his criminal activities in South Africa. He buys and sells weapons. He is interested in vibranium because he can sell it for a lot of money.

Erik Killmonger

Erik Killmonger is also known as Erik Stevens. He is a young American, a killer who has worked for the American government around the world.

*CIA: The Central Intelligence Agency uses spies around the world to collect information for the United States government.

Introduction

The men screamed as Black Panther attacked again and again. The fire from their guns could not touch him. He leaped from one truck to another with the speed of the wind. His body turned in the air like a cat. He clawed and kicked until all the men were on the ground.

Black Panther, a fierce fighter with special powers, is T'Challa, the new King of Wakanda. In this story, he learns where he can find a deadly criminal. Klaue stole from Wakanda and killed many of its people. But it will not be easy to bring Klaue back to Wakanda. At the same time, T'Challa discovers a terrible secret that his father hid from the world. Friends become enemies, and he has to fight a deadly challenger. What will happen? Can T'Challa protect Wakanda from attack? When the fighting ends, will he still be king?

Moviegoers saw T'Challa, the Black Panther, for the first time in *Marvel Studios' Captain America: Civil War*, when his father was killed. Black Panther then joined the Avengers to find the Winter Soldier. They thought he was an international killer. But before that, Black Panther's country, Wakanda, was already important in Marvel films. The shield of Captain America, another Avenger, is made of vibranium, the strongest metal in the world. This metal is only found in Wakanda. Vibranium was also important in *Marvel Studios' Avengers: Age of Ultron*. Ultron used it to make a body, and from this a new Avenger, Vision, was formed.

In these stories, vibranium has always existed. Millions of years ago, a piece of vibranium fell to Earth and hit an area of Africa. It changed the ground and plants around it. Five tribes came together to live there. The country of Wakanda was born. But there was always war between the tribes until, in a dream, one warrior was shown a purple, heart-shaped plant. It gave him special powers. He became very strong, and very fast, and was the first Black Panther. Four tribes agreed that he could be their king. The Jabari tribe refused. They went to live alone in the mountains.

The Wakandans used vibranium to become technologically the most successful country in the world. But they decided to hide their success from other countries.

There will always be people who want to use power in different ways. Some want to use it to become rich. Some want to use it to kill. Others want to use it to become leaders. And some want to use it to help others. How should the Wakandans' vibranium be used? Black Panther must decide.

In Africa, and other parts of the world, some countries and large companies use materials and people from poorer countries to make them richer. The people from those poorer countries suffer as a result. In this story, the Wakandans start to think about how we can all become strong together.

Oakland, California, 1992

◆————————————————————————————————◆

The boy catches the ball, runs, jumps, and drops it into the basket.

"Yes!" he shouts, and the boys happily continue their game outside. They do not look up at the evening sky. High above them, two strange, green-blue lights shine through the clouds. A spaceship moves quickly across the sky toward the apartment building behind the playground.

A few minutes later, there are three sharp knocks on an apartment door. The two men in the room immediately hide the guns that were on the table in front of them.

"Is it the Feds*?" one asks.

"No, James," the other says slowly. He has a bad feeling.

James looks through the door's spy hole. "It's two women with spears!" he says, surprised.

"Open the door! They won't knock again." His friend knows about these visitors. They always get what they want.

James opens the door.

The women are tall and strong, and dressed as warriors. They walk in past James. "Who are you?" one of them asks the other man.

* the Feds: people who work for the FBI (Federal Bureau of Investigation). This organization fights serious crimes in the United States. It also finds information to protect Americans at home and sometimes in other countries.

"I am N'Jobu, Prince of Wakanda." He opens his mouth to show a shiny, blue vibranium-powered tattoo. Immediately, the women hit the floor hard twice with their spears, and the room goes dark. When the light returns, there is another person between the two women. He is tall, and dressed head to foot in black. Around his neck is a circle of golden claws. It is Black Panther.

"My King." N'Jobu goes down on his knees in front of Black Panther— T'Chaka, the King of Wakanda.

Black Panther takes off his helmet and smiles at his younger brother. "It is good to see you."

"How is home?" N'Jobu asks.

The King's face grows serious. "Not good. There has been an attack." He touches his wrist and a hologram forms in the room. It shows a man with wild eyes, a lined face, and a gun. "This man, Ulysses Klaue, stole a large amount of vibranium from Wakanda. He killed many of our people when he was escaping."

The hologram shows fires and clouds of dark smoke. People are running and screaming.

"This thief, Klaue, he had help. He knew where to find the vibranium," King T'Chaka says quietly. He looks into his brother's eyes. "Tell me, baby brother. Why did you help this enemy?"

"I did not ..."

T'Chaka's eyes burn. "You were not the only spy we sent here. Show him who you are, Zuri!" "James" opens his mouth and shows the same tattoo.

"What?" N'Jobu cannot believe it. He turns to Zuri. "I thought you were my friend! You lied to me!" He pushes him angrily.

Zuri's eyes are cold. He brings a glass bottle to T'Chaka. The strange, blue light of stolen vibranium shines brightly inside it. It proves N'Jobu's crime.

T'Chaka feels sad. He loves his brother, but he is the protector of Wakanda. "Prince N'Jobu, return immediately to Wakanda!" he orders. "You will tell our people of your crimes."

Outside, the young boy's eyes are pulled toward the sky. He forgets the ball game. His friends follow his eyes, and their mouths fall open. They watch the strange, green-blue lights jump across the sky. What are they? Where are they going? Why were they here?

An Old Enemy Returns

Many years later

News of the King's death went all around the world: "King T'Chaka of Wakanda was killed last week during an attack at a U.N.* meeting. Wakanda is one of the poorest countries in Africa, in the heart of rain forests. Its new king will be T'Challa, the son of T'Chaka."

As he watched the news on his Wakandan spaceship, above Nigeria, Prince T'Challa had tears in his eyes. He carried the picture of the attack clearly in his mind. He saw again the fire and the flying glass from the windows. He saw himself leap to push his father to the floor. He felt again the pain of being unable to save him.

"My Prince, we can see the trucks now," the warrior next to him said, and T'Challa brought himself back to the present.

Below the ship, a line of trucks was moving slowly through the dark trees. T'Challa picked up his Black Panther helmet and prepared to go down. The warrior, Okoye, reached for her spear.

"You don't need to come, Okoye," he said. "I can do this and bring back Nakia."

* U.N.: the United Nations. This is an international organization that tries to bring countries together. This, they hope, will stop wars.

"Fine," the warrior said and gave him six small Kimoyo stones. They were made of vibranium. "But I know that you loved her. Don't freeze when you see her again!" she added with a smile.

"Freeze?" T'Challa smiled, too. "I never freeze!" he said and jumped through the hole in the spaceship floor. As he fell toward the ground, he threw the stones. They traveled through the night air and hit the sides of the trucks. Their power stopped the trucks immediately.

What is happening? the drivers asked themselves. *Are we under attack?*

The men were afraid of an enemy in the dark. They stood with their guns, ready to shoot. In the last truck, a man was guarding a group of women. He did not realize that one of those women was preparing to join the attack. Her name was Nakia, and she was a Wakandan spy. The men were taking women to sell. Her job was to stop them.

One driver was braver than the others. He lifted his gun and moved slowly through the trees. *What was out there? Was it dangerous?* Suddenly, his light shone on a black shape. He saw fierce eyes and shining claws, and then something hit him hard in the chest. The powerful animal knocked him into the air and back to the truck.

The men screamed as Black Panther attacked again and again. The fire from their guns could not touch him. He leaped from one truck to another with the speed of the wind. His body turned in the air like a cat. He clawed and kicked until all the men were on the ground.

Nakia knocked down the guard in her truck. Then, she ran to face Black Panther.

He looked at her and the world stopped for a second.

"Hey," he said softly. "I wanted to ..."

Suddenly, someone screamed. Another guard was pointing his gun at one of the women from the truck. *WHOOSH!* A spear cut through the air, and the guard lay on the ground.

Okoye stood over the body and looked at T'Challa. "You froze," she said, and walked away. *Men*, she thought.

"Why are you here?" Nakia said angrily. "I didn't need your help. I'm doing my job!"

"My father is dead," T'Challa said quietly. "I will become king tomorrow. I want you to be there."

Nakia could see the pain in his eyes. She turned to the women. "You are free now. Go home to your families."

T'Challa, Nakia, and Okoye jumped into the spaceship, and seconds later it lifted into the air like a great, shining, blue bird. It flew away into the night sky.

It traveled over sands, snowy mountains, and green trees until finally Okoye smiled. "We're home," she said, and the ship slowed and dropped closer to the ground.

It seemed that they were moving toward a thick forest. Then, they broke through the hologram like a stone hitting water. The air was full of blue electricity and the trees disappeared. They were flying over a modern city with apartment blocks, houses, rivers, and parks. They were in Wakanda's capital, the home of the kings.

T'Challa's mother, Ramonda, and his sister, Shuri, welcomed them when they landed.

T'Challa's mother, Ramonda, and his sister, Shuri, welcomed them when they landed.

"Did he freeze?" Shuri asked Okoye. Okoye was standing with the other guards.

The tall warrior smiled. "He did!"

T'Challa looked down, and Shuri laughed.

"Your father and I are very proud of you, T'Challa," Ramonda said softly. "You know he is here with us. He always will be. But now it is your time to be king."

The head of the Museum of Great Britain in London was a busy woman, but she liked to speak to the visitors. When a young man asked for her, she went to him with a cup of coffee from the museum café in her hand.

"Where's this one from?" He was pointing at a metal head in a glass case.

"Ah—that's from Benin, from the 1500s," the woman said, and drank some of her coffee. *How long will this take?* she thought. She needed to do some work.

"And this one?" The man pointed at an old metal tool.

"That's much older, and it's also from Benin." She looked at her watch.

"No." The man shook his head. "O.K., British soldiers took it from Benin—but it was stolen from Wakanda. It's vibranium."

The woman's eyes showed surprise, and he laughed. "Don't worry," he said. "I can look after it for you!"

Who was this man? Was he dangerous? The woman started to turn to the museum guards, but suddenly she felt a sharp pain in her stomach. Her face went white.

The young man put his mouth close to her ear. "You have all these guards," he said. "But you don't check what you put inside your body."

She looked down at the coffee in her hand. Then, she cried out and fell to the floor.

"Quickly! Help! Get a doctor! She's sick!" the man shouted.

After this, things happened very quickly. Other museum visitors were pushed out of the room to let two health workers in. They went straight to the woman and seemed to check her. But then they stood up, turned, and shot the woman and the guards around them. They were robbing the museum.

One robber put his hand against the case with the vibranium tool in it. The glass shook as lines of blue electricity passed through it, and it broke. He took out the metal tool, and in his hands, the old metal fell away from the outside of it. Inside, it was clearly vibranium.

There was a crazy light in the robber's blue eyes as he turned to the young man. "You're going to be a very rich boy," he laughed. His voice showed that he was from South Africa. "I've already sold it!"

"The Wakandans will find you," the man said.

"Good!" Ulysses Klaue laughed. "I'll be ready for them."

There was a crazy light in the robber's blue eyes as he turned to the young man.

The Challenge

Wakandans in bright purple, green, red, and gold clothes covered the mountainside above the blue water of the Challenge Pool. The sound of their songs and their feet on the rocks filled the air. It was a great day. Everyone wanted to see T'Challa become their king.

Below them, long, flat boats moved slowly across the water. They carried T'Challa's family and leaders of four Wakandan tribes. The warriors danced and hit their spears on the wooden floors. It was beginning: the ritual that every future Wakandan king had to face.

With his face and body painted blue and white, T'Challa stood in the shallow water. In his hands were a spear and a shield. He was ready. If another warrior challenged him, he had to fight. He was nervous as he looked up at the excited faces of his people.

Zuri, the leader of the ritual, lifted a gold cup high in the air.

"This will take away the power of the Black Panther," he said. The drink was made from the special Wakandan heart-shaped plant. T'Challa drank, and felt it burn in his blood. The Black Panther power left him, and he was again an ordinary man.

"Now," Zuri shouted to the crowds. "Does anyone challenge T'Challa to be king?"

"Our tribe will not challenge today!" Four times the crowd heard the words from the four tribes. No challengers! Thousands of voices shouted his name. T'Challa looked up at his people, excited about the future. He was king!

But suddenly, a roar cut through the noise of the crowds. Men with painted faces and spears came through an entrance in the mountainside, and the people grew silent. These men were Jabari, the mountain tribe. The first, a big man with angry, black eyes, looked at T'Challa. The Prince knew him. It was M'Baku, the leader.

"I challenge T'Challa!" he cried. "Our tribe has watched you from the mountains. We've seen you turn away from your old life. You mix with people from outside Wakanda. And the vibranium technology is in the hands of a child." He pointed at Shuri. T'Challa's sister was a very intelligent scientist. "And, do you want a king who could not even save his *father?*"

"I accept your challenge." T'Challa's voice was quiet, but cold.

There was silence and the crowds could feel the electricity in the air. Zuri knew that the ritual had to continue. But he also knew that M'Baku was strong and brave. He was afraid for the Prince.

"Begin the challenge," he said.

Warriors from both tribes made a circle around the two men in the water.

Slowly, the people on the mountainside started to hit their sticks on the rocks. The noise was joined by the crash of metal on metal, as spears hit shields. The men in the water were fighting for their lives. Both men fell. Both men stood to fight again. The water danced wildly around them. Then the crowd gave a great cry as M'Baku knocked T'Challa's spear from his hands.

"Where is your power now?" M'Baku laughed. "You are only a boy. You cannot be a king!"

Bravely the Prince tried to fight back without a weapon. But then he felt a sudden, hot pain in his chest. It was M'Baku's spear. T'Challa moved back weakly and almost fell. His eyes became cloudy, and the shouting and singing seemed far away. But then he heard his mother's voice.

"Show him who you are!" Ramonda cried.

T'Challa shook his head to clear the clouds. Now, he could hear the crowd repeating his name. He heard the sound of the sticks on the stones. He felt the love of his people.

"*I am Prince T'Challa!*" He shouted the words, and they made him strong. He pulled the spear from his chest. With the roar of a panther, he leaped at M'Baku, and together the men went down. The crowd watched as they got closer and closer to the rocks. Arms and legs crashed in and out of the water. Who was winning? Then, T'Challa locked his leg around M'Baku's neck.

"Accept defeat!" he shouted over the noise of the water. M'Baku refused. T'Challa's leg pressed harder. "Accept defeat!" he cried again. "Your people need you!"

Finally, M'Baku weakly gave him the sign to stop. The people went wild. Their prince was the brave winner and now he was their king.

There were tears in Zuri's eyes as he put the circle of gold claws around T'Challa's neck. "My King," he said proudly.

T'Challa smiled and crossed his arms over his chest. The colors of purple, gold, red, and green danced over the hillside as the crowd repeated the words, "Wakanda forever!"

Later, in an underground room deep in the mountain, T'Challa was prepared for the second ritual. He lay in red sand and was given another drink by Zuri. This time, the purple plant brought back the power of the Black Panther.

"This will take you to the Land of the Fathers." Zuri spoke softly. "T'Chaka, come to your son."

T'Challa's heart slowed as the plant carried him into a dream. Zuri covered the sleeping man's body with the red sand.

Pictures started to run through T'Challa's head. He saw his father again, softly touching the faces of T'Challa the child, then T'Challa the boy, and finally T'Challa the man. Now, he saw himself crying and holding his father's dead body in the black smoke. He watched himself take the ring of Wakanda from his father's finger. He remembered how empty he felt.

Slowly, the pictures from the past disappeared, and his body became lighter. He was in a strange land of grass and trees. The trees were dark against the blue light of evening, and the sky was alive with purple fire and silver stars. In one dark tree, large black panthers watched him carefully.

Slowly, one panther climbed down from the tree and its shape changed. T'Challa was standing in front of his father.

"You are a king now," T'Chaka told his son.

Accept defeat!" he cried again. "Your people need you!"

"You must keep honest men with good hearts close to you"

"Tell me ..." T'Challa looked into his father's eyes. "Tell me how I can best protect my people."

"It will be hard," he said. "You are a good man. It is difficult for a good man to be king. You must keep honest men with good hearts close to you."

And then he was gone. T'Challa's heart jumped in his chest as he woke from the dream. He sat up in the red sand, and Zuri held his shoulders.

"Be calm, be calm," Zuri said.

T'Challa smiled. "He was there, Zuri," he said. "My father, he was there."

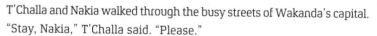

T'Challa and Nakia walked through the busy streets of Wakanda's capital.

"Stay, Nakia," T'Challa said. "Please."

Nakia smiled, but shook her head. "My work is outside Wakanda. There are people who have nothing. We should use our technology to help them."

"But if the world knows about vibranium and our technology, our way of life will change." This was an old disagreement between Nakia and T'Challa.

"Wakanda is strong. We can help other people *and* protect our country."

T'Challa laughed. "You have very strong opinions, Nakia. Too strong for a queen!"

Nakia smiled. "Queens *should* have strong opinions," she said. Then, she added quickly, "Maybe!"

T'Challa was at his friend W'Kabi's farm in the country. There, W'Kabi kept white rhinoceroses in a field. T'Challa told him about Nakia's ideas.

"No!" W'Kabi had a different opinion. "If we let people into Wakanda, they will bring their problems." Then, he added, "But we can help them by fighting their governments."

T'Challa shook his head. War was not Wakanda's way.

Suddenly, a hologram grew in T'Challa's hand. It was Okoye. She smiled. "We have some interesting news!" she said.

It was T'Challa's first meeting as king with the tribal leaders. He was nervous but excited as they listened to Okoye.

"An old vibranium tool was stolen from a museum yesterday," the warrior explained. "We have just learned that Ulysses Klaue plans to sell the vibranium to an American buyer. This will happen in South Korea tomorrow night."

"Yes!" T'Challa stood up. "Klaue has escaped us for too long. I will go to Korea!"

"My parents were killed in Klaue's attack on Wakanda." W'Kabi stood, too. He needed to destroy this man. "Take me with you. We can kill him together!"

"No, W'Kabi, I need you to stay here. You must protect Wakanda," T'Challa said.

W'Kabi was not happy. *It should be me*, he thought. *I want this killer to suffer at my hands.*

"Then promise me this." W'Kabi looked at his king. "When you find Klaue, kill him. Or bring him back to us. He must not escape again."

"I promise," T'Challa said quietly. "I will bring him here!"

Klaue Is Caught

Shuri could not stop smiling. This was so exciting! *There is going to be some dangerous action,* she thought. *I can play my part!* She had a lot of wonderful new equipment to show her brother. It could help him in South Korea and maybe even save his life.

The young scientist welcomed her brother proudly into her laboratory. T'Challa looked around at the modern tables, and the walls made of glass and silver metal. He and Shuri were deep inside the mountain where the vibranium was found. Through the windows, they could see the dark rock, shining with blue and purple light.

"Who are you taking to Korea with you?" Shuri asked.

"Okoye and ... Nakia."

Shuri laughed. "Is it a good idea to take your old girlfriend?"

"It will be fine," her brother smiled. "And you will also be able to help us—remotely," he added. Shuri's smile got bigger. *Yes!* she thought. At last—some action for her, too!

"I have sent a special car already to South Korea," she told him. "And with one of these vibranium Kimoyo stones, I can drive it remotely from here! And you must see this!" Excitedly, Shuri pulled her brother to one side of the room. "If you are going to fight Klaue, you will need the best suit. Look at these." They were standing in front of some Black Panther suits. One was his old suit, with a helmet.

"Old tech," Shuri said. Then she copied T'Challa's deep voice. "'Er—everyone is shooting at me, but wait! I'll put on my helmet!'"

"But this one ..." She pointed at a simple neck circle of silver claws. "Touch it."

T'Challa touched it, and a complete Black Panther suit grew around the claws.

"Now, kick it!"

T'Challa knocked the suit across the room. They could both see new lines of shining purple across the chest.

"See that!" she said. "The material of the suit keeps the power of the attack. It uses that power against your attacker next time. Try again." Shuri began to film with her phone. "For my records," she explained, with a smile.

T'Challa kicked the suit again. This time it didn't move, but T'Challa was thrown back by its power and up into the air. The King landed on his back.

"Stop recording!" he ordered his sister. Shuri laughed.

The three Wakandans were strange visitors to the Korean street that night. Tall, strong, and clearly foreign, they were very different from the usual customers buying fish and other street food. But T'Challa, Okoye, and Nakia were not there to buy food. They had a more serious job—to find Klaue.

Nakia spoke to a Korean woman and soon a door opened in the house behind her. A man checked them for guns, and the Wakandans went inside. After the noise and smells of the street, the inside of the building was surprisingly different. It was a place for people with a lot of money. Under low, gold lights, beautifully dressed men and women moved between games tables on the floor below them. Some were talking, some were drinking, and many were watching the action on the tables. The smell of money was strong. It was an illegal club where rich people tried to get richer. It was also a place where a lot of money was lost.

"Klaue is here," T'Challa said. "I know it."

While Okoye stayed on the upper floor, T'Challa and Nakia went down the stairs to the main games area. Nakia held T'Challa's arm, and he smiled. *It's a good feeling*, he thought, *to have Nakia so close*. But then, he remembered why they were there. He looked around. Where was Klaue?

Suddenly, he heard Okoye's voice in his ear. "Look up!" she said. "Americans. Three."

Nakia looked behind her. "Five," she said.

"Six," T'Challa added. An American was playing at one of the tables. It was a face from T'Challa's past—a man called Everett K. Ross, from the CIA. What was he doing here? Was he the American buyer? Why?

T'Challa joined Ross at the table. He reached across the American to place money on the game. "You are buying from Klaue?"

The CIA man was surprised. How did the King of Wakanda know about this meeting? Ross continued to play. "I'm here to do a secret job for the American government. This is not your business, T'Challa. You should leave *now*."

"Klaue *is* my business," T'Challa said calmly, and moved some more money on the table. "And he is going to walk out of that door with me."

But Ross had his own plans. "I need Klaue." He looked around the room. Where was the man? He needed T'Challa to go. "He has some information that we need. After this is finished, you and I can talk."

"No," T'Challa said. "Klaue will come with me—tonight!"

Outside the club, four big, black cars arrived, and Ulysses Klaue jumped out of one. The Korean woman welcomed him like an old friend, and he and his men walked into the club. No gun check. No questions. Everyone

knew him. He looked around the club with a big smile. Someone here had a lot of money for him. It was dangerous, but Klaue loved danger. And his men were there to protect him.

Okoye saw him immediately. "Klaue is here," she said. "And he's brought men. A lot of men. They all have guns." T'Challa quickly moved away from the American and turned his back.

Klaue's crazy eyes searched the room and found Ross quickly.

"The money?" He smiled widely at the CIA man and touched his shoulder like a friend. Or a possible enemy.

Ross knew the danger of agreeing to meet this criminal. He looked toward the door, and a man brought him a silver case. "Have you got the vibranium?" Ross asked quietly.

Klaue reached into a bag and pulled out something heavy. It was covered in cheap brown paper.

Suddenly, T'Challa heard Okoye's voice. "They've seen me!" she said urgently. One of Klaue's men was moving toward her.

Okoye was Wakanda's greatest warrior for a good reason. She was fast and deadly. In seconds, she pulled out her hidden spear and hit the man. Two more of Klaue's men attacked her, and her spear lifted and dropped at an impossible speed. Finally, it swept one attacker off his feet. He flew through the air and crashed onto the tables below.

Klaue immediately fired at Ross. The CIA man used the silver case as a shield and fell to the floor. Quickly, the club filled with the sound of gunfire as Klaue's men attacked the Americans and the Wakandans. People screamed and ran for the doors.

WHOOSH! Okoye's spear cut through the air. Another man was dead. Nakia was fighting, too, and was almost as fast as Okoye. Then, she found

"The money?" He smiled widely at the CIA man and touched his shoulder like a friend.

a gun, and soon more men were on their backs.

Now, it was a real fight. Okoye leaped down to the tables with a war cry. Her spear shone silver in her hand. The warrior was a killing machine. *THUD!* More men fell. Next to her, T'Challa was fighting three men at the same time.

Then, he saw Klaue on the top floor and ran after him. "Murderer!" he shouted.

The robber turned and fired, but nothing happened. His gun was empty. But his smile didn't die. It grew bigger. He was clearly enjoying the fighting and the fear around him. He lifted his left arm.

"You look like your father!" he said. Then, he lowered his arm. T'Challa saw that his hand and lower arm weren't real. The arm opened, and a gun appeared. Vibranium fire burned through it as Klaue fired.

T'Challa jumped back and pulled a table between them. Paper money flew through the air.

Klaue laughed crazily as he watched the money falling. "Hey!" he shouted excitedly. "It's raining!"

Then, he was running out of the club with his men. At his car, he looked back. His face was shining like a child's. "Wonderful!" he said. "That was wonderful!"

He jumped into the car. "Let's go!" he shouted at the driver. "Go! Go! Go!" And the four cars roared down the city street.

Nakia and Okoye left the club first. As they jumped into their car, Okoye threw a Kimoyo stone onto the roof of another car. Now Shuri could drive it remotely for T'Challa.

"Shuri!" T'Challa shouted as he ran down the road. "Now!"

In her laboratory in Wakanda, Shuri climbed into a hologram of T'Challa's car. *Yes!* she thought. Now, she was really part of the adventure. She started the car, and it roared into action. She guided it remotely down the Korean city street.

T'Challa touched the claws at his neck, and the Black Panther suit formed around him. As the car moved past him, he leaped onto the roof. He kept his head low against the wind, ready for a very wild ride.

The four black cars in front of the Wakandans drove away. But which

"I'm going as fast as I can," his sister shouted back.

car was Klaue's? T'Challa followed one car, and Nakia followed another. They raced through the city streets, moving in and out of the traffic.

"Faster, Shuri," T'Challa shouted.

"I'm going as fast as I can," his sister shouted back. Soon, T'Challa was close to his black car. He leaped onto its roof and reached one strong arm down to the driver's window. He pulled the man out and threw him on the road. Shuri felt the car drive over his body. *CRUNCH!* But it wasn't Klaue.

Now Nakia and Okoye were behind *their* black car. The passenger started shooting at them, but Shuri's special car was made of vibranium. The gunfire couldn't touch it.

Okoye shook her head sadly. "Guns," she said. "Old tech." Then, she climbed out of the window and onto the roof of the car.

"Careful!" Nakia cried. But Okoye moved her body like a dancer. She found her position, then lifted back her arm to throw. Her silver spear reached its goal, and the black car crashed. But this wasn't Klaue's car either. They continued driving. There were more black cars in front of them.

The third one was racing across a bridge with T'Challa close behind it. The wind was cold in his face and loud in his ears.

Shuri brought his car to the side of the black car, and he jumped across. With a great cry, he lifted one end of the vehicle. It flew into the air. *CRASH!* It landed on its roof. Another black car was out of action. But again—no Klaue.

T'Challa jumped back onto Shuri's car. There was only one black car left and this *was* Klaue's. Nakia and Okoye were getting nearer. The prize was close. But Klaue had his vibranium arm weapon. He fired out of the car window and hit the Wakandans' car. Vibranium fire hit vibranium metal and the gunfire won. The car fell to pieces, and the women stood alone on the road. Okoye's eyes were black with anger. It was hard for a warrior to accept defeat.

Another car stopped next to the women. "Jump in," Everett K. Ross said.

Now, T'Challa was behind Klaue. "Faster, Shuri, faster," he shouted. And there was Klaue, the enemy, right in front of T'Challa. He could almost touch him.

Klaue was ready with his gun. *T'Challa*, he thought. *Good!* It was time for the new king to meet his dead father again. Blue fire shot from his arm, and immediately T'Challa's car was destroyed.

"*Ow!*" Shuri said as the hologram disappeared. She sat down heavily on the floor in her room.

But that was not the end. T'Challa leaped onto Klaue's car. He landed lightly, and his strong Black Panther claws cut into the body of the car. He lifted it easily and threw it into the air. It turned over and over, and finally crashed down onto the road. Klaue fell out of the broken window. He was still smiling, and pointed his arm gun at the Wakandan king.

T'Challa walked slowly toward his enemy. This was the time. Now, he could keep his promise to W'Kabi and kill this animal. "In Wakanda," he told the killer, "we never forget."

Klaue was not worried. He knew that his vibranium weapon could kill anyone or anything. He laughed, and his gun shot blue fire again. *Goodbye, Panther*, he thought. But T'Challa did not fall. He continued walking. For a second, Klaue's smile left his face.

T'Challa pulled Klaue's weapon off his arm and threw it on the road. "Look at me, murderer!" he cried. His Black Panther claws reached out for the man's neck. Klaue was the reason for so many deaths in Wakanda. He had to pay. He had to die.

A voice stopped him. "King! No!" It was Nakia. "The world is watching," she said, and then T'Challa saw the crowds. There were people all around them. They were holding up phones and taking photos.

"Let's go," Ross said from his car.

T'Challa dropped his arms, and Ulysses Klaue looked up at him. The crazy light was in his eyes again, and he smiled.

T'Challa Learns His Father's Secret

Ulysses Klaue was inside a locked room and tied to a chair. But he did not seem to worry. He was laughing and talking to the walls, to himself, and to his enemies outside.

"We must not let Klaue talk to Ross alone," Okoye said fiercely in Wakandan. "Klaue knows too much about vibranium."

But Ross refused to let T'Challa anywhere near Klaue. "You can watch through this window," the American said. "And then you're going home."

When Ross went into the room, Klaue was singing. His face was covered in blood from the car crash, but he did not look or sound like a prisoner.

Suddenly, the mad light left his eyes. "Don't listen to those Wakandans," he said. "I'm more useful to you than they are."

Ross sat comfortably in front of him. "I'm interested in the weapon that was on your arm," he said. "Where did it come from?"

Klaue looked at the mirror. He knew that it was a window for the people outside the room. "Ask your friends," he smiled. "Wakanda is more than a country of farmers with pretty animals and trees and rivers. It is built on vibranium. You know vibranium?" He moved his head as close to Ross as possible.

"Of course. It's the strongest metal in the world."

"Exactly," Klaue agreed. There was nothing crazy about him now. His voice was quiet and serious. "Wakanda is full of it. They use it in their clothes, it powers their cities, their tech, and ... their weapons."

Ross laughed. "But Wakanda is a poor country. And you *stole* all their vibranium!"

"I stole ..." Klaue thought this was very funny. He sat back in his chair, laughing wildly again. But only for a few seconds. He stopped suddenly, and his eyes went cold. "I took a small piece. They have a mountain full of it. Ask your friend about his suit, about his claws. Ask him what they're made of."

Ross looked at him. Was this true? Could he believe a crazy killer like Klaue? He left the room.

"How much more vibranium are you hiding?" he asked the Wakandan king.

Suddenly, a loud noise shook the building, and Klaue's room filled with smoke. Through it, T'Challa could see a great hole in the wall. A young Black man climbed into the room and moved through the smoke toward the mirror. He calmly lifted a gun and started shooting. Behind him, two other people lifted Klaue in his chair and carried him out through the hole.

"Get down!" Ross shouted, as pieces of the mirror and gunshots flew everywhere. For a few seconds, the room was full of noise, fire, and smoke and then, the shooting stopped. The young man leaped back through the hole in the wall. T'Challa followed, running. His Black Panther suit formed around him. He had to return Klaue to Wakanda. He had to keep his promise.

The young man jumped into a white van and turned. He fired at T'Challa again and again, and Black Panther was thrown on his back. The van drove away, but not before T'Challa saw something strange. Around his neck, the young man was wearing a silver ring. It was a ring that T'Challa knew well.

"My King," Okoye shouted from the building. "Quickly!"

Nakia was on her knees next to Ross. The man's face was white, and his eyes were closed.

"He jumped in front of me," Nakia explained. "He saved my life. But he was shot in the back. I don't think he will live."

"Wait." T'Challa took a Kimoyo stone from his wrist and placed it carefully into the small hole in Ross's back. "This will keep him safe while we take him back to Wakanda. He saved Nakia's life. We have the technology to save *his*. We cannot let him die."

The white van drove into a yard that was full of old and broken machines and parts of planes. In the middle of the trash was one plane that was not old or broken. It was waiting to fly the van's passengers to the United States. Klaue started to climb in.

"On the way, you can leave us in Wakanda," the young American said. He and his girlfriend were behind Klaue.

"No. You don't want to go there!" Klaue wasn't really listening. He was already thinking about his next plans.

"Yes, I do." The young man pulled out his gun and shot the plane's pilot.

Klaue looked crazy, but he could think and act very quickly. He immediately pulled the girl in front of him, and put his gun against her head.

"You'll be O.K.," the young American told the girl softly. But his eyes were empty. He lifted his gun again and shot her, too.

Then, Klaue ran. He tried to hide between the broken planes, but the young man calmly followed him. Another shot and Klaue fell. He looked down at the circle of blood on his chest. He knew that he could not get up.

"The Wakandans will kill you." His voice was weak.

The young man stood over him. He lifted his arm and showed Klaue lines of small, dark circles all along it. "Each of these is a kill," he said.

"You're crazy." Klaue started to smile. "You'll always be an outsider in Wakanda."

The young man looked at him and slowly opened his mouth. He showed the criminal his tattoo.

Klaue shook his head. "Ah," he said. "And I thought you were only a crazy American." Then, his laugh was cut off by a final gunshot.

Zuri was planting the purple, heart-shaped plants when T'Challa found him. The underground area was quiet and calm, but T'Challa's heart was going fast. He needed some answers from Zuri.

"Zuri," he said, "what happened to my uncle?"

Zuri stood up, but said nothing. The question was not a surprise. He was carrying a secret that was heavy inside him.

"The story is that he disappeared." T'Challa moved around the plants. "But there was a man today ..." He turned to Zuri and lifted his hand. "He was wearing a ring, the same as this one on my finger."

Zuri could not look at his king. "That is not possible."

"Do not tell me that it is not possible." T'Challa was getting angry. "He helped Klaue escape. He was wearing this ring, my grandfather's ring!"

Zuri moved to put more plants in his basket.

"Tell me, Zuri. What really happened?"

Zuri lifted his head. There was a deep sadness in his eyes. "I promised your father—the King—to say nothing," he said quietly.

T'Challa's voice was shaking. "*I* am your king now!" he cried.

Carefully, Zuri put down his basket. The plants gave a purple light to the room. Usually they made him calm, but not today.

He started to tell his story. "Your uncle was working for Wakanda in the

"I promised your father—the King—to say nothing," he said quietly.

United States. He was a War Dog, one of Wakanda's secret police. Your father sent me, too, to watch him. I was like—a spy. Your uncle fell in love with an American woman, and they had a child. Your uncle learned many things in the United States. He saw people who were very poor. Many had terrible lives. And not only in that country. All around the world, African people were suffering. Your uncle wanted to change things. He wanted to use vibranium weapons to defeat the bad governments. He thought that Wakanda could lead the world, in a better way. But he knew that your father did not agree. So your uncle, N'Jobu, helped Wakanda's enemies."

"No!" T'Challa moved toward him, but Zuri held up his hand.

"It's true," he continued. "He helped Klaue to steal the vibranium from Wakanda. When your father came to our apartment in the United States, your uncle realized that I was a spy. He became angry, and pointed his gun at me ... and your father killed him." There were tears in Zuri's eyes as he remembered the night. "He killed his own brother to save my life." His voice was shaking. "I promised your father to say nothing about that night—ever."

For a few seconds, T'Challa couldn't speak. The story took away his words. His kind, fair father ... a killer?

Suddenly, he understood everything. "And the child?" He asked his last question.

Zuri dropped his head. "We left him there." He spoke very quietly, but T'Challa heard every word clearly. "We had to keep the secret."

The sun was low in the sky over the Wakandan hills. The young American pulled a heavy bag across the grass and left it at W'Kabi's feet.

"What is this?"

"A little gift," the young man smiled.

W'Kabi opened the bag, and Klaue's dead face looked up at him.

W'Kabi lifted his eyes to the young man's. The air around them was suddenly very calm. People, animals, trees—everything seemed to stop moving.

"Who are you?" he asked.

Everett K. Ross woke up in a strange, white room. *Where am I?* he thought. He got off the bed and touched his neck. He remembered guns and a terrible pain in his back. But his hand was dry—there was no blood. *How? And who's that?*

Shuri was working at a computer. She smiled. "Everett K. Ross," she said. "Fighter pilot and now CIA. You're in Wakanda."

"But ..." Ross couldn't understand. "How long ago was Korea?"

"Yesterday," Shuri replied.

"No." He shook his head. "I was badly hurt. It takes a lot longer than a day to get better."

Shuri laughed. "Not in Wakanda," she said. "We have the technology."

Ross looked around at all the glass and computers. Then, he walked slowly toward a big window. Through the window, he saw great rocks with a strange, blue light. He also saw lines of silver that moved in circles at great speed around the rocks. They were like a railroad of lights, and they climbed up and up. *This is a dream*, he thought.

"These train things ...?" he asked Shuri.

"Ah, those are railroad cars," she explained. "Vibranium is too dangerous to move at fast speeds. I found a way to stop its power for a short time. While it's moving."

"That's vibranium on those trains?"

"There's vibranium all around us." Shuri laughed again. "That's how I made you better!"

Then, a hologram of Okoye's head formed in her hand. "A man has arrived in Wakanda," Okoye said. "He says that he killed Klaue. I'm sending you his picture."

Shuri and Ross looked at the picture of the young man.

"Is he Wakandan?" Shuri asked Okoye.

Ross knew the face. "No," he said slowly. "He's one of ours. Erik Stevens."

Later, he explained to T'Challa: "He was a soldier in Afghanistan. He killed people like he was playing a video game. He earned the name Erik *Killmonger*. Now, he belongs to a special group of soldiers who kill secretly. Politicians, leaders ..."

T'Challa looked carefully at the eyes of the young man in the picture. They were completely empty. *My father made this man a killer*, he thought, *and now Wakanda is going to suffer.*

Erik Killmonger walked fearlessly into a meeting of the tribal leaders, with W'Kabi.

"I have brought the body of Ulysses Klaue to you," he told the leaders, and his mouth lifted in a half-smile. "Something that your king could not do!"

T'Challa leaped to his feet and went to the American. "There is only one reason why I don't kill you here." He spoke quietly, but fiercely. "I know who you are. What do you want?"

Erik Killmonger turned to the leaders again. "I want to be king!" he said simply.

"There is only one reason why I don't kill you here." He spoke quietly, but fiercely.

Everyone laughed.

Erik Killmonger spoke again, but louder. "Look at you!" he said. "You all have good lives. But there are many people around the world whose lives are much harder. Wakanda should use its vibranium weapons to free them all!"

"Wakanda does not make wars," T'Challa said. "We want to keep our people safe. And we want to make sure that people like you can never get vibranium!"

Ramonda was getting angry. "Tell him to go, T'Challa," she shouted. "We refuse his request!"

Erik Killmonger smiled. "It is not a request!" he said. "Ask me. Ask me who I am!"

"You're Erik Stevens," Shuri cried. "You're a killer!"

"That's not my name, Princess," Erik Killmonger said. "Ask me, King. Ask me my name!"

T'Challa turned his back on the American. "Take him away," he ordered. But then, the voice of one of the tribal leaders gave Erik Killmonger the question that he wanted:

"Who are you?"

Erik Killmonger lifted his head proudly. "I am N'Jadaka, son of Prince N'Jobu," he shouted in Wakandan.

Suddenly, everyone started speaking and shouting at the same time. But it was the American's stage now. His words came like shots from a gun: loud, fast, and deadly.

"I found my father's dead body. There were Black Panther claws in his chest. You ..." His black eyes burned into T'Challa's. "You are the son of a murderer."

W'Kabi held up the American's ring. "It's true!" The noise stopped. No one spoke, no one moved.

"I challenge T'Challa, to be King of Wakanda!" Erik Killmonger's words fell like stones in the silent room.

T'Challa looked at the ring. This man had the blood of kings, but he was also a dangerous killer. What should he do? The room waited for T'Challa to answer.

Finally, he spoke. His eyes met Erik Killmonger's. "I accept your challenge," T'Challa said slowly.

A New Black Panther

The mountainside above the Challenge Pool was empty. There were no Wakandans in bright clothes. No one was shouting or laughing. There were no songs or dancing feet—only warriors with faces of stone. They were in a line around the pool. Ramonda, Shuri, and Nakia stood next to them. They watched as Zuri started the ritual. Their fear for T'Challa was clear on their faces. There was a deadly purpose in the challenger's eyes.

The ritual began. The warriors hit the rocks with their spears, and Zuri gave his king the drink made from the heart-shaped flower. It took away the Black Panther powers, and T'Challa stood next to Erik Killmonger, an ordinary man again.

Erik Killmonger took off his shirt. His skin had the record of hundreds of deaths. "I lived all my life with this hope," he said calmly. "I was waiting for this time. I worked, I lived, I fought. I *killed* to be here today." He looked into the eyes of his enemy. "In the U.S., in Afghanistan, in Iraq ..." he continued. "I killed everywhere so I could be here ... to kill *you!*"

"The challenge can begin." Zuri spoke quietly, and stepped back.

With a loud cry, the men lifted their weapons, and knife crashed heavily onto shield. From the start, T'Challa knew that he was fighting for his life.

The younger man was stronger, his speed was faster, and his knife and spear screamed through the air. He kicked and leaped with the skill of a cold killer. But T'Challa answered the challenge. His love for his country and his people made him stronger and braver. He gave a great roar, and his shield knocked Erik Killmonger onto his back. But the younger man stood up again quickly, his hate giving him more purpose than ever. Again, his knife shone silver in the sun. T'Challa was getting tired and slow to defend himself. And then, the challenger's knife moved through the air faster than eyes could follow. Suddenly, there was blood on the King's face, then his arms, his stomach, and finally his legs. The pain brought T'Challa to his knees, and Erik Killmonger lifted his heavy knife for one last time.

"For my father!" he screamed. But his knife crashed onto the metal of Zuri's spear.

"*I* am the reason your father died, not T'Challa," Zuri cried. "Take *me!*"

Erik Killmonger smiled. "I'll take *both* of you!" he said, and he drove his knife into Zuri.

"No!" T'Challa reached out weakly to his old friend. The water was red with their blood, but he tried to stand. Erik Killmonger easily knocked him down again and turned to the warriors.

"Is this your king?" he shouted.

Again, T'Challa tried to stand, and again he fell. Erik Killmonger kicked his enemy one last time, and this time he stayed down. Erik Killmonger lifted T'Challa's body over his shoulder and carried him to the rocks. There, the water crashed down hundreds of meters into the river below. For a second, Erik Killmonger held T'Challa high in the air. Then, he dropped

the body over the rocks.

Erik Killmonger turned to the warriors and T'Challa's family, and held his spear high in the air.

"Now," he shouted, "I am your king!"

Nakia took Ramonda's hand. "Quick!" she said urgently. "We have to go now! I'll get Ross. But Okoye will not come. Her job is to protect the king—even a bad king."

Nakia, Ramonda, and Shuri ran along a path into the mountain.

Zuri's assistant put the circle of claws around Erik Killmonger's neck with shaking hands. The young man's eyes shone. This was his dream at last. He was King of Wakanda, and soon the Black Panther. With vibranium and the Black Panther powers, he could do anything he wanted.

The warriors crossed their arms over their chests. It was the sign that they were in front of their king, their new king.

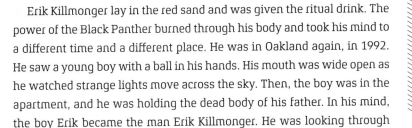

Erik Killmonger lay in the red sand and was given the ritual drink. The power of the Black Panther burned through his body and took his mind to a different time and a different place. He was in Oakland again, in 1992. He saw a young boy with a ball in his hands. His mouth was wide open as he watched strange lights move across the sky. Then, the boy was in the apartment, and he was holding the dead body of his father. In his mind, the boy Erik became the man Erik Killmonger. He was looking through his father's book when he found a ring.

"This tells you that you must go home." Suddenly, N'Jobu was next

"I am the reason your father died, not T'Challa," Zuri cried. "Take *me!*"

Soon, fire filled the room, and the beautiful flowers became black smoke.

to him. "When the sun dies at the end of the day, Wakanda is the most beautiful place in the world." He smiled. But then, his face became sad. "I am afraid you will not be welcome. I was wrong. I didn't take you back when you were younger. Now, we are both lost."

Suddenly, Erik Killmonger was in the ritual room again. A terrible fear went through him like electricity, and he jumped to his feet. He looked around wildly, ready for an attack.

Then, he remembered where he was. He looked around and saw the purple plants. There were hundreds of them, small and heart-shaped. They existed so more kings could become Black Panthers.

But I am the king. There will be no more kings after me, he thought. *I must destroy them.*

"Burn them," he shouted. "Burn them all!" Soon, fire filled the room, and the beautiful flowers became black smoke. Erik Killmonger watched. Now he was sure. He was the last Black Panther.

No one noticed Nakia's hand reach out from the dark. She picked and hid the final purple plant.

"In my country," Erik Killmonger told the tribal leaders, "there is no one to help the poor people. But Wakanda can."

He looked around at the old, wise faces. "We have spies—our War Dogs—in every country," he continued. "We will send them vibranium weapons." His voice grew fiercer. "The people will kill the leaders and their children. It will be a new world. And Wakanda will lead it!"

The four people on the mountain path—Ramonda, Shuri, Nakia, and Ross—left the warm Wakandan sunshine behind. The path climbed higher to a place where the wind carried snow. They were going to the home of the mountain tribe, the Jabari. They stopped at the entrance into the mountain.

Ramonda was worried. "I don't like this," she said to Nakia. "If we take the heart-shaped plant to M'Baku, will we have bigger problems?"

Nakia held up her hand. "Listen!" They heard the soft fall of feet on the snow and a strange, deep animal noise: *Huh! Huh!* Soon, they were circled by Jabari men. The men did not speak, but pushed the group through the entrance. They followed a dark path until they came to a large room in the mountain. After the shining, white snow, it was dark and scary underground.

M'Baku was sitting with two guards at his side. He did not seem surprised to receive this visit from his enemies.

"My son was murdered in a ritual challenge!" Ramonda told him.

"If the fight was fair, then it was not murder," the mountain leader said, with a half-smile. "It was defeat."

"Great M'Baku ..." Nakia showed him the purple plant. "We are here to offer this to you. Only you can help us. We have to stop the outsider."

M'Baku looked at it for a short time. *What's he going to do?* Ross thought. Then, the big man stood up. "Come with me," he said.

He led them along another dark mountain path to another large room. In the middle of it, there was a bed.

Ramonda's hands flew to her face. "Impossible!" cried Nakia. In front of them, a body was lying on a bed of ice. It was T'Challa. His eyes were closed, but he was alive.

"One of my men found him in the river," M'Baku explained. "He brought him to me. The ice is keeping him from death."

"Quick, Nakia," Ramonda said. "The plant." She mixed the ritual drink and poured it into her son's mouth. "Fathers!" she called. "Give him life!" The women covered T'Challa with snow.

This time, for T'Challa, it was not night in the Land of the Fathers. A pale light hung over the trees and grass. T'Chaka smiled to welcome his son. Behind him, there were kings from other times.

"Come home, T'Challa. Join us," he said softly.

"Why, Father, why did you leave the boy?" T'Challa asked.

T'Chaka looked at him sadly. "I chose to hide my mistake. I chose my people."

"You were wrong! All of you," T'Challa said angrily. "You were wrong to turn your backs on the world. You didn't want anyone to discover our secret. But it stopped you from doing the right things!" His eyes were wet with tears, but his voice grew stronger. "No more!" He shook his head. "I cannot stay here with you. I cannot rest while _he_ is king. He is a terrible man—but _we_ made him. I must now make things right again!"

T'Challa woke suddenly. For a few seconds, he had no idea where he was. He only knew that he was very cold. Then, he saw the friendly faces around him and smiled. "Does anyone have a coat?" he asked.

"Erik Killmonger has full power," Shuri told T'Challa later. "He has all our warriors, all our vibranium, and all our technology."

"He will send weapons around the world," T'Challa said quietly. "I must return."

Shuri smiled and took something from her coat. She put the circle of silver claws around T'Challa's neck. "Black Panther lives. And I will fight at his side."

"And I will," Nakia said.

"And I," said Ross.

T'Challa turned to M'Baku. "I thank you," he said simply. "Will you help us?"

"A life for a life. I have paid that now," the warrior said. "But, no. Your kings have never come here before. We will not help you."

In Wakanda, deep inside the mountain, machines were putting piles of weapons on fighter planes. The planes flew up and out into the blue sky.

"We'll start with London and New York," Erik Killmonger told W'Kabi, as they watched one fly away with its deadly passengers.

Suddenly, the plane became a ball of fire in the air. It crashed to the ground, and clouds of black smoke poured from the burning metal. A dark

She mixed the ritual drink and poured it into her son's mouth.

shape climbed onto the back of the plane. Black Panther stood clearly against the fire.

Okoye's heart jumped in her chest. "He lives!" she cried.

"N'Jadaka!" T'Challa shouted. "I never accepted defeat! As you can see, I am not dead!"

"*I'm* king now!" Erik Killmonger shouted. "Get the planes in the air," he ordered his men. "We will continue!" Erik Killmonger turned to W'Kabi. "Kill him!" he said.

"You cannot!" Okoye cried. "The challenge is not finished!"

But W'Kabi didn't want to listen. Erik Killmonger was his king now. It was Erik Killmonger who brought him Klaue's body, not T'Challa. The old king was weak and bad for Wakanda.

"Get him!" he roared. His men pulled out their long knives and with a war cry ran toward T'Challa.

"I never accepted defeat! As you can see, I am not dead!"

The Final Fight

Okoye hit the ground with her spear. *THUD!* It was a sign for the other warriors. Immediately, they took their fighting positions. "Your heart is so full of hate that you can never be a true king," she shouted at Erik Killmonger. "Protect the King!"

Some guards ran to help T'Challa. Some stayed with their leader.

Erik Killmonger smiled and touched the claws around his neck. *I am the Black Panther*, he thought. *Nothing can hurt me.* The warriors leaped at him with their spears, and he knocked them back easily. But they didn't stop. They attacked from all sides. Feet, spears, and arms rained down on Erik Killmonger at impossible speeds. But the vibranium suit made him faster and stronger. He moved like the wind. Soon, he held a warrior in front of him, his knife at her neck. He laughed as her blood painted the stones red.

Okoye screamed, and the warriors attacked even more fiercely. Their spears shone silver, lifted, and fell. Finally, the spears locked around Erik Killmonger's chest. The power of the vibranium in all the spears pushed him to his knees.

"Get the claws!" Okoye cried. "Quickly!" She could feel the power of the Black Panther pushing back at them. Then, suddenly the spear lock was broken, and the warriors were thrown high into the air.

Shuri, Nakia, and Ross ran into the science laboratory, and Shuri picked up some weapons. She had a plan.

"Here." She put a circle of Kimoyo stones around Ross's wrist. "You'll need these for me to talk to you." Then, she touched a switch. Immediately, there was a hologram of a fighter plane seat in front of them.

"What?" Ross didn't understand.

"Nakia and I will steal one of the *real* planes. *You* must fly it remotely." Ross's face went pale, but Shuri smiled. "I'll guide you. It's like riding a bike! You are a great pilot, and I've made this plane hologram American style!"

The women left him and ran up to the flight area. More planes were flying away with their weapons. Shuri threw a vibranium Kimoyo stone at one of the planes that was still on the ground. It hit the side. Now it was theirs. Ross could fly it remotely.

"Get into the hologram!" Shuri cried to Ross in the laboratory. "You must shoot down all the planes in the air. Those weapons must not leave Wakanda."

In the hologram, Ross tried to be calm. "Right," he said quietly. "Here we go!" He pulled a stick, and the real plane lifted into the air.

"Right," he said quietly. "Here we go!" He pulled a stick, and the real plane lifted into the air.

W'Kabi leaped onto the back of the first animal and rode through the fighting.

T'Challa was defending himself against W'Kabi's men, but a plane was also shooting at him from the sky. Suddenly, W'Kabi was in front of him. T'Challa's power threw him back.

"Stop this, W'Kabi!" T'Challa shouted to his old friend. "Stop this now!"

W'Kabi looked at him coldly. He was fighting to take Wakanda's future along a different path. He was sure that it was the right one. He climbed to the top of some rocks and lifted something to his mouth.

A low, deep sound came from W'Kabi's mouth. Soon, a big, dark shape was moving through the clouds of smoke above the crashed plane. The great head and body of a rhinoceros jumped over the broken metal, and the ground shook with its weight. More animals followed. They were all covered with metal helmets and body protection. They were all ready to kill. W'Kabi leaped onto the back of the first animal and rode through the fighting.

Ross could see an enemy plane in front of him. "What do I do?" he said into his microphone.

"Shoot them down, smart boy!" Shuri shouted in his ear.

"O.K." Ross pulled another stick. *BANG!* Fire shot from his guns, and the weapons plane crashed into the river below. "Yes!" he cried.

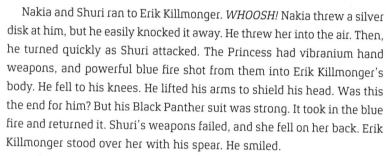

Nakia and Shuri ran to Erik Killmonger. *WHOOSH!* Nakia threw a silver disk at him, but he easily knocked it away. He threw her into the air. Then, he turned quickly as Shuri attacked. The Princess had vibranium hand weapons, and powerful blue fire shot from them into Erik Killmonger's body. He fell to his knees. He lifted his arms to shield his head. Was this the end for him? But his Black Panther suit was strong. It took in the blue fire and returned it. Shuri's weapons failed, and she fell on her back. Erik Killmonger stood over her with his spear. He smiled.

In the middle of the fighting, T'Challa heard his sister's cry. With all the power of the panther, T'Challa leaped and knocked Erik Killmonger back. Together, the two men fell through a wide hole that reached down deep into the center of the mountain.

T'Challa felt the wind sing in his ears as he fell down past the blue rocks of vibranium and past the flight areas. He landed on the train lines on his back, and all the air left his body. Then, Erik Killmonger fell on the ground next to him. Both Black Panthers leaped up, ready to fight again. Gold claws and silver claws screamed through the air as they fought fiercely. Each man was fighting for his dream.

I cannot defeat him, and he cannot defeat me, T'Challa thought. *We are both Black Panthers*. Then he had an idea. "Shuri," he shouted into his microphone, "switch on the train on the bottom line!"

"But that will stop the power of the vibranium—and the power of your suit. You will become weaker!" she cried.

"But he will, too," T'Challa said.

The vibranium train started to run, and both men's helmets and claws disappeared. Their Black Panther powers were gone while the train passed.

On one side of the train, Erik Killmonger shook his head. "I don't need a suit to kill you!"

T'Challa tried to talk to him. "You hate all those people. But with your plans, we will become the same as them. You will destroy the world—and Wakanda, too!"

"The world took everything away from me," Erik Killmonger said. "It took everything that I loved." When the train stopped, the Panther powers returned. He leaped across the lines again.

An electronic voice suddenly spoke in Ross's ear. "Closing hologram," it said.

Slowly, parts of his plane hologram began to disappear.

"What's happening?" he cried.

"They're attacking the laboratory!" Shuri shouted. "Get out now!"

The electronic voice spoke again. "The hologram is losing power."

The Princess had vibranium hand weapons, and powerful blue fire shot from them into Erik Killmonger's body.

Ross was a good pilot. He knew what he needed to do. "Put me in again," he said calmly.

W'Kabi's men were winning. They formed a circle around the warriors and lifted their vibranium shields. Okoye and her soldiers were locked inside a bright, shining, blue ring. Their spears couldn't break it.

"You have three seconds to put down your weapons," W'Kabi shouted from the back of his rhinoceros. "One ... two ..." But he did not reach three.

Suddenly, the sound of heavy feet and deep animal noises broke the silence. A great arm lifted W'Kabi by his neck. M'Baku stood proudly in front of his men from the mountains.

"See!" he cried. "The Jabari are here!" And he threw W'Kabi at the blue vibranium shields.

"Continuing to lose power," the electronic voice said. "Weapons are failing."

Ross could feel that the plane was weaker. But there was one more weapons plane to shoot down. He had to get it before it left Wakanda. "Shuri—there's one more plane! I'm slowing. What can I do?"

"Cross your arms over your chest," she told him. Ross did it. "Now, push your arms out quickly. It will turn on the hologram again for a short time."

The electronic voice spoke, "Starting in five—four—three ..." But the plane was dropping through the air like a stone. "Two—one."

And it stopped, a few meters above the ground.

Ross pulled a stick, and the plane lifted and raced toward the final weapons plane. He fired for the last time, and saw the weapons plane crash. Then, the hologram disappeared, and Ross hit the floor of the laboratory.

The Jabari were strong fighters, and soon they were winning. But W'Kabi was on his rhinoceros again, and with a roar he rode straight at M'Baku. *The Jabari leader must die*, he thought. *The fight will be ours.* But Okoye stepped in front of the mountain tribe warrior to protect him. Then, something very strange happened. The rhinoceros suddenly stopped. It dropped its great head and touched her face softly.

W'Kabi climbed off the animal and started to pull out his knife. But Okoye was faster. Her spear pointed at his chest.

"Can you really kill me?" W'Kabi asked, with a smile.

Okoye's eyes were hard and cold. "For Wakanda?" she asked. "I can!"

W'Kabi looked around. His men were defeated. He went on his knees and threw his knife on the ground. It was the end of his fight.

But the fight under the ground continued. It was close. Both Black Panthers were strong; each of them had the power of vibranium. Then, another train passed, and their powers disappeared again. Erik Killmonger moved quickly. He brought his spear to T'Challa's neck.

"This is the end for you, Cousin," he smiled.

But T'Challa hit his enemy hard in the stomach and knocked his arm

Both Black Panthers were strong; each of them had the power of vibranium.

back. The spear flew up in the air. T'Challa caught it, turned, and pushed it into the young man's chest. The fight was finished.

Erik Killmonger fell to his knees. He knew that he was dying. He looked around at the blue rocks and up at the open sky far above them.

"My dad told me about Wakanda." His voice was weak. "He promised to show me." Then, he laughed. "I was only a kid. I believed his stories!"

T'Challa felt very sad. He could see the child in the dying man's eyes. He was paying for their fathers' mistakes. There was one last thing that he could do for the American.

The true King of Wakanda carried his defeated challenger to the elevator. It took them up through the mountain again to a wide shelf of rock. From there, they could see out across the valley and the fields. The sun was a red ball in the evening sky as it dropped slowly behind the hills.

Erik Killmonger watched it for the first and last time. The orange light was warm on his face. "It's beautiful," he said simply.

"Maybe we can make you better," T'Challa said, but Erik Killmonger shook his head.

"Why?" he asked. "To put me in prison? No, give my body to the ocean. My African fathers jumped from ships. For them, it was better to be dead." Suddenly, he pulled the spear from his chest and blood poured down his body. He closed his eyes in pain, and then his face grew calm.

The sun disappeared, and shadows reached across Erik Killmonger's dead body.

The orange light was warm on his face. "It's beautiful," he said simply.

Let's Change

It was a bright, new day in Wakanda. People filled the busy streets in the city. All was calm again.

T'Challa stood with Nakia. "Thank you for helping me and my family, Nakia." T'Challa's words were simple, but his eyes said much more.

Nakia smiled. "You do not need to thank me," she replied.

T'Challa kissed her softly. "Please stay," he said quietly. "I have a plan. You can stay, and you can also do your work."

Oakland, California, one year later
The boy catches the ball, runs, jumps, and drops it into the basket.

"Yes!" he shouts, and the boys happily continue their game.

Two people are watching them.

"Why have you brought me here," Shuri asks her brother. "When you said California, I thought—Disneyland!"

T'Challa points at the apartment block next to the playground. "This is where our uncle died. It's where our father killed him."

Shuri's face grows serious. She reads a sign on the wall. "They are pulling it down. Good," she says.

"No." T'Challa shakes his head. "I have bought this building. And that building. And that one." He looks at two more tall blocks. "I am going to build a Wakandan Center. Nakia will help the people, and you will organize a science information program."

"You're joking!" Shuri's eyes are wide with surprise.

T'Challa does not reply. He touches one of the Kimoyo stones around his wrist and a hidden Wakandan spaceship slowly appears in front of them on the playground.

The boys stop their game and watch. Then, with open mouths, they run to look.

"What's that?" one shouts.

"It looks like a spaceship!" another cries.

One boy doesn't run with the others. "You!" he calls to T'Challa. "Is this yours?"

T'Challa says nothing.

The boy looks carefully at the strange man with the silver claws around his neck. "Who are you?" he asks.

United Nations, Vienna

T'Challa is speaking to a group of leaders from around the world.

"My name is T'Challa, son of T'Chaka. I am the King of Wakanda. For the first time, we want to tell you about our technology. We will not continue to watch the world from the shadows. We cannot. We must not. Brothers and sisters can live and work together. When there are problems, mindless people build walls. But wise people build bridges. We must find a way to live together, like one single tribe."

"I have a question," one leader asks. "What can a country of farmers offer the rest of the world?"

At the back of the group, Everett K. Ross smiles.

Activities

Chapters 1-2

Before you read

1 Look at the Word List at the back of the book. Check the meanings of new words in the dictionary, then name:

  a something that we use a basket for
  b an animal that is fierce
  c an animal that doesn't have claws
  d an animal that can leap
  e a weapon that fires
  f a place where you can see a spear
  g a time when we need to wear a helmet

2 Find Who's Who? at the front of the book. Work in pairs.

  a Look at the pictures. Do you know any of these people from another movie? If you do, what do you know about them?
  b Read about the people. Who will help Black Panther in this story? Who will fight against him? Who will die? What do you think?
  c Who is the most interesting person, in your opinion? Why?

3 Read the Introduction and answer these questions.

  a Have you seen any films about the Avengers? Who is your favorite Avenger? Why?
  b What do you think T'Challa's father hid from the world?
  c How do you think Wakanda hides its technology from the world?
  d Do you know any examples of how rich countries use materials from poorer countries?

While You Read

4 Match the names and the descriptions. Use one name twice.

Klaue   N'Jobu   T'Chaka   Zuri

a the man in the apartment with James ....

b N'Jobu's brother ....

c the man who stole vibranium from Wakanda ....

d James's real name ....

e the man who helped Klaue steal the vibranium ....

5 Circle the words that are wrong. Write the correct words.

a T'Challa was killed during an attack at the U.N. ....

b Okoye is carrying a gun. ....

c The special Kimoyo stones destroy the trucks. ....

d The drivers are going to kill the women in their trucks. ....

e Nakia is happy when she sees T'Challa. ....

f Wakanda is hidden by clouds. ....

g The museum visitor is interested in things from Asia. ....

h The robbers take a vibranium helmet. ....

After you read

6 Work with two other students. What will happen in the apartment after King T'Chaka tells his brother to return to Wakanda? Have the conversation between T'Chaka, N'Jobu, and Zuri.

7 Work with another student. Have this conversation.

Student A: You were a visitor in the museum when the robbers arrived. What did you see? How did you feel?

Student B: You are a police officer. Ask the visitor questions about the robbery. What happened? Can they describe the robbers?

Chapters 3-4

Before you read

8 Look at the Word List at the back of the book. Complete these sentences with the best words.

a The warrior carried a .... to protect her body.
b The parents .... their children to a football game.
c Some people can turn on lights in their houses .... when they are away.
d .... are found in Africa and Asia. The largest males can weigh 2,400 kilos.
e The crowd gave a .... when the football player got a goal.
f We have science lessons in a .... at school.

9 Read the titles of Chapters 3 and 4, and look at the pictures. Discuss these questions.

a What do you think the challenge is? Who challenges who?
b How do you think Klaue is caught? Where? Who catches him?

While you read

10 Who is speaking? Write the names.

a "Does anyone challenge T'Challa to be king?" ....
b "And the vibranium technology is in the hands of a child." ....
c "And, do you want a king who could not even save his *father?*" ....
d "Show him who you are!" ....
e "T'Chaka, come to your son." ....
f "Queens *should* have strong opinions." ....

Now compare your answers with another student's. What is the speaker talking about? What does he or she mean?

11 Answer these questions.

a Why does W'Kabi want to kill Klaue?

....

b How will Shuri use a vibranium Kimoyo stone?

....

c Why does Ross want to buy the vibranium?

....

d Why does a fight start in the club?

....

e Why doesn't T'Challa kill Klaue?

....

After you read
....

12 Whose opinions are these? Who do you agree with? Explain why.

a Wakanda shouldn't use its weapons to fight other countries.
b Wakanda should use its technology to help people in other countries.
c Wakanda should help people in other countries by fighting their governments.

13 Discuss how you think these people feel and why.

a M'Baku after the challenge
b Everett K. Ross after the fight in the club
c W'Kabi when he hears that Klaue is still alive

14 Work with another student. Have this conversation.

Student A: You are in the club when the fight starts. Phone a friend. Say what is happening. What can you see? What can you hear and smell? How are you feeling? What are you going to do?
Student B: You are at home, when your friend calls from the club. Ask questions.

15 Imagine that you are in the crowd at the end of Chapter 4. You take a photo and send it to your friends. What does the photo show? Write the message that you will send with the photo.

Chapters 5–6

Before you read

16 Discuss this question: What do you think will happen to Klaue now?

While you read

17 Put these sentences in the right order, 1–8.

a Klaue is taken away in a van. ....

b Erik Killmonger talks to the tribal leaders. ....

c Ross is shot in the back. ....

d Ross wakes up in Shuri's laboratory. ....

e Zuri tells T'Challa about his father. ....

f Ross asks Klaue questions in the prison room. ....

g Erik Killmonger takes Klaue's body to W'Kabi. ....

h Klaue is killed. ....

18 What happens next? Write a sentence.

a Zuri stops Erik Killmonger's knife with his spear.

....

b Erik Killmonger carries T'Challa to the rocks.

....

c Erik Killmonger wakes up from his dream in the Land of the Fathers.

....

d Ramonda asks M'Baku for his help.

....

e T'Challa wakes up from his dream in the Land of the Fathers.

....

f A plane with Wakandan weapons crashes in front of Erik Killmonger and W'Kabi.

....

After you read

19 Work with another student. Erik Killmonger has just given Klaue's body to W'Kabi. Continue this conversation:

W'Kabi: What is this?
Erik Killmonger: A little gift.
W'Kabi: Who are you?

20 Imagine you are the man who found T'Challa in the river. Tell your story.

21 Discuss these questions. Give reasons for and against.
a Was T'Chaka right to leave the child in the United States?
b Is Okoye right to stay with the new king?
c Is W'Kabi right to fight with Erik Killmonger?

Chapters 7–8

Before you read

22 What do you think will happen to these people?

Erik Killmonger   M'Baku   Okoye   Ross   T'Challa   W'Kabi

While you read

23 Are these sentences right (✔) or wrong (✗)?
a Okoye fights Erik Killmonger alone. ◯
b Ross flies a fighter plane from a hologram in the laboratory. ◯
c W'Kabi rides a horse through the fighting. ◯
d T'Challa stops Erik Killmonger killing Shuri. ◯
e T'Challa and Erik Killmonger fall down into Shuri's laboratory. ◯
f Shuri turns off the trains on the line. ◯
g M'Baku's men help fight W'Kabi's men. ◯
h Ross shoots down all the planes before the hologram fails. ◯
i Okoye hurts W'Kabi with her spear. ◯
j Erik Killmonger dies inside the mountain. ◯

24 Answer these questions. Make notes in your exercise book.

a Why is everything calm again in Wakanda at the beginning of Chapter 8?

b What is T'Challa going to do with the buildings that he has bought in Oakland?

c Why has he bought *these* buildings?

d What will Shuri do in Oakland?

e How will Wakanda under King T'Challa be different in the future?

After you read

25 Discuss these questions.

a T'Challa says, "When there are problems, mindless people build walls. But wise people build bridges." What does this mean? Do you agree? Think of examples of "walls" and "bridges."

b Rituals are important in the story. Give some examples of rituals in your country. Are they important to you, or to other people? Why (not)?

c Imagine another person in a story with the special powers of an animal, like Black Panther. What can he or she do?

Writing

26 You are the young boy with the ball in the playground in Chapter 1. Write a message to a friend about the lights in the sky. What did you see and hear? What do you think they are? How did you feel?

27 After the museum robbery, the police want to find Klaue. Write a description of him to put in the newspapers.

28 Write about Erik Killmonger's life. Is the end of his life surprising? Why (not)?

29 What is vibranium? Where does it come from? Explain why it is very important in this story.

30 Write about Wakanda. Write about the history, the people, the language, the capital, other parts of the country, and the country's leaders.

31 Choose two of the people in the story and compare them. In what ways are they similar? How are they different?

32 You are a reporter for the *Wakandan News*. Write a report of the final fight.

33 You are T'Challa. The new Wakandan Center in Oakland is going to open soon. Write an email to your mother and tell her about it. What will it do? Why? When will it open? What can people do there?

34 Write about the story. Did you like it? Why? Is it a good book for others to read?

35 Work with another student. There is going to be another Black Panther story. What will it be about? Who will be in it? Will there be some new people? Write a plan for the story.

Word List

basket (n) something that we carry things in—eggs, for example. People throw a ball through a basket in some sports.

challenge (n/v) something that tests your skill. If you challenge someone to a game of tennis, you want to win.

claw (n/v) sharp things at the end of some animals' feet. Cats, for example, have a claw on each of their eighteen toes.

deadly (adj) very dangerous

defeat (n/v) If you accept defeat, you have lost. If you defeat someone, you win.

fierce (adj) strong, angry, and frightening

fire (v) to shoot a gun. **Gunfire** is repeated shooting.

helmet (n) a strong, hard hat that protects your head

hologram (n) a special type of photo that doesn't seem flat

laboratory (n) a special room or building where scientists work

lead (v) to walk in front of other people. A leader is the most important person in a group, organization, or country.

leap (v) to jump quickly and very high

museum (n) a building where we can see important historical or scientific things

panther (n) a large, wild cat. Black panthers are found in Asia and Africa.

power (n) the ability—sometimes unnatural—to do something. A **powerful** person is very strong or important.

remotely (adv) from far away

rhinoceros (n) a large African or Asian land animal with a very thick skin

ritual (n) actions that are repeated at important times, for example by followers of a religion

roar (n/v) a very loud, deep noise, like the call of a large, wild cat

shield (n/v) something that you hold in front of your body. It protects you from attacks.

spear (n) a long stick with a sharp point that was used, in the past, for fighting

tattoo (n) a word or a picture that is drawn on your body

technology, tech (n) the use of modern science in machines and equipment. We all see technological changes during our lifetimes.

tribe (n) a group of people in one area, like a big family, that have the same language and way of life

warrior (n) a brave, strong fighter

weapon (n) something that you fight with, like a gun or a knife